A Child's Book of

Composers

By Hannah Hoyt

Tables of Contents

I.

Franz Liszt Meets Beethoven

This book will introduce you to new friends. They all lived 200 years ago, and their world was different than ours. But they left their music behind, and their stories.

The first friend we will meet is named Franz Liszt. Franz was born in Hungary in 1811, and soon his family moved to Austria. Franz was an only child, with blond hair that got browner as he grew older, and blue-green eyes. His father worked as a clerk for Prince Esterhazy. At the prince's court, people wondered who the next great musician would be. No one expected it would be the clerk's son Franz! But if they had seen Franz's face the first time he heard and saw a piano, they might have guessed it. Little Franz had tears in his eyes and said it was the most beautiful sound he had ever heard. So his father gave him piano lessons, and Franz became wonderfully good at the instrument.

Because Franz was so talented, his parents wanted the best education for him. So they moved to a big city called Vienna where he could find good teachers. One teacher was Mr.

Salieri, who taught Franz how to compose music. And Mr. Czerny taught him piano.

Franz was eleven years old when his highly esteemed teacher Czerny introduced him to his hero, Ludwig von Beethoven. Franz wanted to meet Beethoven more than anything, but the composer was getting older, and was deaf. He couldn't hear anymore, and instead his friends had to write their conversations down so he could read what they were trying to tell him. He was not usually nice to people.

For a long time, Czerny told Beethoven about Franz, and asked Beethoven to hear Franz play. But Beethoven didn't like prodigies and for a long time refused to hear Franz. Finally, he was persuaded by Czerny's persistence.

"Then for goodness sake, bring the little rascal." Beethoven said.

It was one morning about ten o'clock when Franz and his teacher Czerny entered the two small rooms of the Schwarzspanierhaus, where Beethoven lived. Franz was somewhat embarrassed – but Czerny kindly encouraged him. Beethoven was sitting by the window at a long narrow table working. For a moment he looked at them both with a serious face. He said a couple of quick words to Czerny but turned silent as Czerny signaled to Franz to go to the piano. Now,

Beethoven would not be able to hear Franz playing, but he could see the notes on the piano, and feel the music rumble through the floor.

First Franz played a small piece of Ries, one of Beethoven's students. When he had finished, Beethoven asked if he could play a fugue by Bach. Franz chose the C minor fugue from The Well-Tempered Clavier.

"Can you transpose this fugue?" Beethoven asked.

That was a hard request. Transposing meant playing the same song higher or lower on the piano…and to do that you needed to play completely different notes to make it sound like the same song. And a fugue — a song with four different melody lines at the same time — was hardest of all to transpose.

But Franz could do it. After the finishing chord he looked up. Beethoven's deep glowing eyes rested upon him – but suddenly a light smile flew over his otherwise serious face. He approached Franz and stroked him several times over his head with affection.

"'Well – I'll be blowed." he whispered. "What a little devil."

Coming from Beethoven, that was a compliment. Franz's courage rose.

"May I play one of your pieces?" He asked boldly.

Beethoven nodded with a smile. Franz played the first movement of Beethoven's piano concerto number 1 in C Major. When he had finished Beethoven stretched out his arms and kissed him on his forehead.

"'You go on ahead. You are one of the lucky ones!" Beethoven said in a soft voice. "It will be your destiny to bring joy and delight to many people and that is the greatest happiness one can achieve."

Years later, Franz Liszt told this story with great emotion: his voice trembled, and you could feel what joy Beethoven's simple words had given him.

"This was the proudest moment in my life – the inauguration to my life as artist." The older Franz Liszt said quietly. "I tell this very rarely – and only to special friends."

Here is some music Beethoven wrote that Franz liked. He knows you will like it too!

1. Beethoven's Fifth Symphony, 1ˢᵗ Movement – This is the most famous piece of music that Beethoven wrote. Can you recognize the little tune being played over and over? Can you sing it or hum it?

2. "Ode to Joy" from Beethoven's Ninth Symphony – Beethoven was working on this grand piece of music when he met Franz Liszt. Even though Beethoven was deaf, he could still hear the music inside his head and write it down for others to listen to!

II.

Becoming the Best You

Adults may say that a person "brings out the best" in someone. They also say to "Be yourself." And you might hear both ideas together: Be the best you that you can be.

Franz may not have understood these things when he was your age. But he must have as he grew older. Do you remember how excited he was when he met Beethoven? After that day, Franz was sure that he would have a wonderful career in music. How do you think Franz felt when things didn't go the way he planned?

12-year-old Franz and his father traveled from Vienna all the way to Paris. Paris had the best music school: The Paris Conservatory. Franz had grand ideas as he traveled. He didn't speak French yet, but he would learn. And if he went to the Paris Conservatory, he would become the musician he always dreamed he would be.

But when Franz arrived at the Paris Conservatory, the headmaster said that Franz could not study there. They didn't admit foreigners. Only students from France.

Franz sat outside the door and cried. His dreams were dashed to pieces. Beethoven had said he was one of the lucky ones. He didn't feel so lucky now.

All Franz could do was stay in Paris anyway, learn French, and study on his own. He took composition lessons from Anton Reicha, a teacher at the Conservatory who also taught some refused children. Like a little girl named Louise Ferranc, who wasn't allowed in because they only taught composing to boys. And like Franz, a Hungarian boy from Austria. When Louise grew up, her composing was so good that the Conservatory hired her to be a teacher! But what happened to Franz when he grew up?

Franz was good at music, everyone could see it. He wrote his own opera when he was thirteen, and the Conservatory performed it. But they still would not let him in. And then when he was sixteen, his father died. He blamed himself for his father's death, because they were on a trip performing Franz's concerts when it happened. Franz went back to Paris to his mother, and to make money, he taught piano lessons to the children of rich families in the city.

Without Franz's father to organize concerts for him and take him to other countries to play, Franz gave up on his music. He didn't think he could do it all on his own. Especially now that he needed to teach to make money. Maybe he didn't think things could possibly get worse for him.

When Franz was seventeen he fell in love with a student of his around his own age. They both loved the same books, and they loved poetry. They would sit together after lessons and talk about their favorite story: Dante's "The Divine Comedy."

But when the girl's father found out about her and Franz, he banished Franz from the house. Franz never got to see her again. Now he had not only lost his father, but the girl he loved too!

Franz shut himself in his room and went to bed. He stayed in bed for days, too sad to come out and face the world. Weeks went by. His mother was worried, but could do nothing for him.

His destiny came charging in with a bang. Student revolutionaries marched down the streets and soldiers shot their cannons. Franz snapped awake at the sound of the fighting outside his window!

When Franz's mother checked on him, he was at the piano again. She smiled.

"It was the guns that woke him." she said.

Franz went out and attended a concert by the famous violin performer Niccolo Paganini. Paganini's playing was so fantastic and inspiring that Franz knew at once what to do.

He would be like Paganini, but on his own instrument: the piano.

For six hours a day for two years, Franz practiced and practiced. He practiced the low notes, and the high notes. He practiced everything in between. And when he started giving concerts again, the public was amazed at his abilities.

It had been hard, but in the end Franz was glad he had forged his own path. If he had gone to the Paris Conservatory, he would have been a musician like everyone else. His playing would have been like everyone else's, and the music he wrote would be like everyone else's too. That would not have been the best version of himself. That path, though it would have been an easier way to success, would not have created the amazing performer and composer he became. The music Franz wrote was full of bold, new ideas. Ideas that may not have been allowed at the Paris Conservatory.

If we had seen that little weeping boy crying outside the Conservatory door, we could have told him (as I hope someone did) that doors often close for a reason. Even though those reasons may not be clear at first.

Are you glad that Franz Liszt grew up to be himself instead of becoming like everyone else? It makes him more fun to talk about, and his music more fun to listen to! What are some things you like to do? How would you feel if you loved playing baseball but you had to grow up playing basketball instead? Would that be a good version of you?

Here's some music Franz wrote that would not have been allowed at the Paris Conservatory:

1. Chromatic Gallop – A gallop is when a horse is running. This song gets faster and faster (until you probably fall off the horse!) This song would not have been fancy enough for the fancy school that rejected Franz. But Franz didn't just want to create fancy things. He wanted his songs to be fun!

2. Mephisto Waltz Number 1 – Mephisto is the name of a bad guy! This song is about him dancing around. Do you like evil villain songs? They can be funny in the movies! Do you think Mephisto is a tall villain or a short villain? Does he have magical powers? Franz thinks so. Do you think Mephisto is a good dancer or not?

III.

Felix and Fanny

Do you have a brother or sister? Do people ever confuse you? Maybe they think your sister drew a pretty picture, but it was really you! Maybe people get your shoes mixed up. Or your names!

This is a story about a brother and sister named Felix and Fanny. They lived in Hamburg, Germany, and their father was a banker. He wanted them to have the best education, so he hired a lady named Marie Bigot to be their music teacher. Ms. Marie knew how to do two important things: she knew how to play piano and how to compose. So she taught Felix and Fanny, and soon something wonderful happened.

Felix and Fanny became good at playing piano and at writing their own music! They gave concerts in their city, and their parents took them on tour to other countries so they could play more concerts. They were called "Prodigies", which is a name for children that can play very hard music.

When Felix grew up, he wanted his job to be in music. So he got a job as the director of a concert hall and he put on concerts all the time. He wrote his own music and published it so other musicians could play it.

Fanny didn't get a job in music, because where Felix and Fanny lived, women couldn't get jobs when they grew up. But they could get married and become mommies. So Fanny became a mommy! But she still wanted to put on concerts and write music. She couldn't do that for her job, but she could do it at home. So she gave concerts at home and invited many famous people to come. Everyone loved Fanny's concerts. And Fanny wrote songs for piano, for singers, for violins, and for church.

Fanny wanted to publish her music, but Felix was afraid what people would think. Their family was important and if Fanny published a song everyone would talk about it. Sometimes people said bad things about Felix's music. He didn't want people to say bad things about his sister's music too.

So Felix and Fanny came up with a secret plan. A music company was publishing a book of Felix's songs. Without anyone noticing, Fanny gave three of her songs to Felix, and

Felix gave the songs to the publishers. They thought that Felix wrote them!

Soon the book of songs was released. Everyone loved them, and no one knew that Fanny had written some of them! Everything was going well, until…

One day Felix was giving concerts a long way away: in England! He gave a concert for Queen Victoria, who was the queen of England and very important. Queen Victoria said that she wanted to sing Felix her favorite song he had written. She sang a song called "Italien." When she finished, guess what Felix said?

He had to tell Queen Victoria that he didn't write that song.

His sister Fanny wrote it! So Queen Victoria found out what a good composer Fanny was. A few years later, Fanny published her very own collection of music.

Felix and Fanny wrote hundreds and hundreds of songs. And even to this day, people still get confused about which of them wrote what! When your grandparents were little, there was a song called "Easter Sonata" and it said F. Mendelssohn on it. Everyone thought Felix wrote it. But a few years ago we all found out Fanny wrote it because she talked about it in her diary.

Felix and Fanny fought like any other brother and sister, but they loved each other very much. And when Fanny died, Felix was so sad that he died six months later. Even though Fanny was three years older than Felix, they were a lot like twins.

Here are some songs Felix wrote that you may like:

1. Midsummer Night's Dream Overture – This is based on a play by Shakespeare and it has fairies and donkeys in it! You can hear the fairies at the beginning coming out to play at night!

2. Wedding March from Midsummer Night's Dream – They play this at weddings sometimes when the bride walks down the aisle. Have you ever heard it? Would you like to walk doing the aisle to it?

3. Fingal's Cave – This is a song about a cave that is near water. Water comes inside the cave and the waves crash against the rocks. It's dark and wet. But it looks magical. The cave is in Scotland, and in Scotland they have stories about mermaids

and sea monsters. Do you think mermaids would like the cave?

4. Violin Concerto in E Minor – This is a song for a violin and orchestra. It's one of the prettiest pieces of classical music and it's difficult to play. If you start the violin right now, you will probably play this song when you're a teenager.

Here are some songs Fanny wrote that you may like:

1. The Year – This is a collection of 12 piano songs: one for each month of the year! You can listen to the song for this month. Does it sound like the weather outside?

2. Prelude for Organ in F Major – Organs are loud and exciting! Sometimes they can sound scary. Does your church have an organ? Does this piece sound happy or scary?

3. Easter Sonata – This one is about Easter! It sounds like springtime and new life. Does it remind you of any animals?

4. Piano Trio – This is a long piece of music for a piano, violin, and cello. This is something three friends can play all

together! Felix and Fanny liked playing music with their friends. What do you play with your friends?

IV.

Lisztomania

Have you ever felt like you're the best at something? Maybe you can run faster than your little brothers, or do math in your head better than your friends, or maybe you read bigger books than your sister does. Has that ever made you feel happy, but made other people jealous?

When Franz Liszt grew up, he wanted to be the best piano player in the entire world. He practiced six hours a day for two years. Then he gave concerts in Paris. Then in Germany. Then in England. Franz gave concerts everywhere, sometimes every day for a week!

Have you heard of a rock star? A musician who is so famous that everyone knows who they are? Franz Liszt was the first rock star. He was the first musician that everyone in Europe and Russia knew about. And just like rock stars today, Franz started making a lot of money.

He bought 32 cravats, which are like bow ties. He had four white horses pull his shiny carriage. He received presents like medals and swords from kings and emperors.

Franz was known as being a kind person, but the fame started to go to his head. He played fast songs even faster so the audience would like how fast he was.

He banged on the pianos harder so the audience would like how loud he was. He banged so hard that he broke piano strings, like rock stars today sometimes break guitars.

The ladies screamed, and fought over his gloves and the leftovers from his coffee. Pictures of Franz Liszt were everywhere. A fever had spread over the world: they called it Lisztomania!

Everyone had Lisztomania, except for Franz's friends.

His friend Clara frowned when she saw him bang too hard on the piano. His friend Robert shook his head when he saw the white horses and carriage. Franz came to Clara and Robert's house for dinner, but he was late. Clara thought he came late because he was famous, and liked making people wait for him.

At dinner, Franz said Robert's music was too much like Felix Mendelssohn's. He didn't have nice things to say about Felix's music either. Finally Robert said "How dare you insult Mendelssohn! He is twice the musician you'll ever be!" Clara was upset too. "I am done with him forever," she said about Franz.

Robert and Clara were not the only ones done with Franz. Franz wrote to his friend Chopin, but he didn't reply. He wrote to Chopin's girlfriend George Sand, who had been his best friend once. "I do not hold your friendship cheap," he wrote. But she didn't reply either. He was all alone, giving concerts in strange countries. Even though he was famous, he wasn't happy.

He realized it had been wrong to let the fame go to his head. It was better to be kind. And it was better to write music from the heart, like Chopin, instead of just writing what his public wanted to hear.

Franz made a decision. He would stop being the best pianist in the world. Instead, he would get a job directing music at a duke's royal court and compose pieces for orchestra. He left behind his 32 cravats, his white horses, and his shiny carriage and went to a little town with a castle called Weimar.

He had lost many friends, but he had one best friend left: Richard Wagner. Franz spend his time helping him. He let Richard stay in his house when he was naughty and needed somewhere to hide. He conducted his operas, and sent him money when he lost his job. Franz learned that being a good friend made him happier than being famous.

Franz read the bible and wrote music for church. He went to Rome and became a priest. Then he came back to Weimar, to a little house with four rooms divided by red, green, and white striped curtains. He settled into his small wooden bed, which was the only thing in the room besides a nightstand and a cabinet of music he had written. He had given away most of his belongings.

Franz had invented something beautiful. It was called a Symphonic Poem. It was a work for a big orchestra, based on a book or a place. The audience was supposed to close their eyes and imagine a scene. He wrote 13 of these Symphonic Poems: one was called "Hamlet" after the Shakespeare play, another was "Festival Bells." There was "Hungary" after his homeland, and "Battle of the Huns" after a painting he had seen and liked.

Now, Symphonic Poems have turned into music for movies. There's music to help you think of "Star Wars" and music to help you think of "Indiana Jones." There's music for you to imagine superhero fights, love scenes, and pirates.

Sometimes when you stop acting like you're the best at something and just focus on doing what you love and being kind to your friends, you can create better things and live a better life.

Here's some music Franz wrote that you may like:

1. A Dante Symphony Mvt. III: Paradiso – This music is supposed to help you imagine a scene in heaven. Do you hear the angels singing? What kinds of heavenly things does it help you to see in your head?

2. Orpheus – This is a Symphonic Poem about the story of Orpheus. Orpheus had a magic harp that made plants and flowers grow. Do

you hear a harp in the music? Orpheus also went on an adventure to the underworld to rescue his wife Eurydice. Does this music ever get dark and scary?

3. The Lake of Wallenstadt – When Franz was still travelling playing piano, he went to Switzerland and found a beautiful, sparkling lake. This is the song he wrote about it. Do you think it was a stormy day or a peaceful, sunny day? Does the water sound like the waves are big or small?

4. Liebestraum (Love Dream) – Franz wrote this song for piano. The melody is played with only the thumbs! The notes in the background are played with the other fingers. What can you do using only your thumbs?

5. Hungarian Rhapsody – Franz lived in Austria but his mother was from Hungary. When he was older he visited Hungary and wrote this song for piano and orchestra based on the music he heard there. Does Hungary sound like a fun place to visit? Sometimes Franz liked to begin his songs with only a melody, and put the other notes in later. Does the piano start with one melody? Or does it come in with many notes at the same time?

V.

Frederic Chopin

Last chapter we learned about Franz Liszt, who was the best pianist in the world. In Paris, where Franz lived, there was another pianist named Frederic Chopin. He didn't bang on pianos like Franz did. He played softly. He and Franz played so many concerts together that they became friends.

This is a story about how Chopin learned that even if you don't like someone at first, they deserve a second try.

It was the end of October, 1836. Franz Liszt wanted to give a concert at his apartment. But who should he invite? He knew he wanted to invite his new friend Chopin, but what about the girl who lived in the apartment below Franz's? Her name was Aurora Dudevant, but everyone called her George Sand. That was how she signed her name when she wrote books and when she wrote for the paper. George loved to write. She also loved to wear pants and a top hat. She loved playing pool and riding horses and going for a swim at midnight and smoking cigars. Everyone in Paris thought she was so odd. They thought her books were full of strange ideas. No one really liked her except Franz.

My friends will all like her if they only got to know her, Franz thought.

The guests arrived. The women wore beautiful dresses...all except George, who wore pants like the men. The men smoked cigars...and so did George. The women chatted, but George didn't talk much, and when she did it was about things that the other women didn't like talking about, like politics.

 Franz played piano, and then his new friend Chopin played piano. George sat in the corner and puffed on her cigar. Chopin played softly, in his special style of speeding up to the high notes and then slowing down. George loved it. She thought maybe she should write an article about Chopin for the paper. "At least I shall try, with great zeal and admiration!" she said.

But Chopin didn't like her. She was different from him. He didn't like cigars, he liked purple flowers. He didn't care about the politics in France, he only thought about Poland and how Russian soldiers had attacked his home there. Chopin didn't like horses or swimming or taking midnight walks. He was always catching colds and going to the doctor, and so he stayed indoors. He liked being polite and proper and following rules. George liked breaking rules!

After the party, Chopin said "How unpleasant that woman Sand is. Is she really a woman? I happen to doubt it."

He wrote home to his parents. "I have made the acquaintance of a great celebrity: Madame Dudevant, who goes by the name of George Sand. Her appearance is not to my liking and doesn't please me at all."

November came, and Franz planned another party. This one was a surprise party for Chopin. Franz gathered his friends together in a big group—including George-- and they picked out food and drinks to bring for Chopin's party. Then Franz led the way down the street to Chopin's house.

They knocked on the door.

Chopin was surprised to see everyone! He was especially surprised that Franz had invited George, who Chopin hadn't really wanted to come. But he lit candles and sat down to play piano. He played music that reminded him of his homeland, Poland. It was beautiful and sad. George loved it. But Chopin still didn't like her.

But Chopin could not ignore George because they were friends with the same people. The next week his friend Charlotte Marliani had a party and George was there too! This time she wasn't wearing pants and a top hat. She wore a beautiful white dress with a red sash. It was the colors of the Polish flag. It dazzled Chopin.

She likes Poland! Maybe we have something in common after all, Chopin thought.

The next time Charlotte Marliani had a party, George and Chopin both came. They talked for a long time. Afterwards, George quietly wrote three words on a piece of paper and passed the note to Chopin. Chopin opened the note. It said "I adore you."

She was in love with him! The next week, they both met again at a friend's house. Chopin improvised on the piano and George sat next to him. The next week, they did the same thing. They talked until midnight.

"From what is happening to me," George said, "I can guess what must be happening in him. We have not seduced each other. We have let ourselves be lifted by a passing wind, which after a few moments swept us away to another land."

"What will come of it? God knows! I am seriously unwell." Chopin said.

He was usually unwell. But George was good at taking care of people. And for many years, George Sand and Frederic Chopin did everything together. They worked together, they took vacations together, they spent Christmas together and lived next door to each other in Paris. They were so much in love that they were like a family, and George's two children became like Chopin's children. Her dog became his dog.

And while George wrote books, Chopin wrote music. He wrote nocturnes, which are songs for nighttime, and he wrote Polonaises and Mazurkas, which are dances from Poland. He wrote a song about the fighting in Poland, called the Revolutionary Etude. And of course he wrote a piano concerto. And while Chopin wrote his music, his dearest George could be found beside him on the piano bench, or sometimes laying under the piano, falling asleep to his beautiful music.

Chopin found out that even if you don't like someone at first, they could become the person you love most in the entire world. You just have to get to know them!

Here's some music Frederick Chopin wrote that you may like:

1. Revolutionary Etude – This piece of music is about the fighting in Poland that started right after Chopin left home. He was so sad that he wasn't there to help with the fighting. Soldiers from Russia took over his city and he was worried that his family died in the fighting. They were okay, but he didn't know that at first. So he

put his feelings into the music so when we listen to it we could feel what he was feeling!

2. The Minute Waltz – The word 'minute' here is supposed to mean 'little,' not a real minute of time. George thought it would be funny if Chopin wrote a song about her little dog Marquis. So Chopin wrote this song, about Marquis chasing his tail! Can you hear the little dog going around and around?

3. Polonaise in A Flat Major – A Polonaise is a dance from Poland. In this dance, the couples parade around the ballroom. Usually the balls were for soldiers and captains in the military, so it sounds official like a military march. Can you try parading around the room to this music?

VI.

Chip Chip's Grrrrrand Concert

One day the pianist Frederic Chopin decided he should give a concert. He was shy and didn't like playing in front of people, so he had not given a concert in seven years. But his friends finally persuaded him.

His girlfriend George Sand was excited when she heard the news, and couldn't wait to tell her friends about it.

"Great, GRANDISSIMO news!" She wrote to her friend Pauline. "Little Chip Chip is giving a grrrrrand concert!"

Before Chopin knew it, his friends had picked a day and a place for his concert, and wanted to print out posters.

"I don't want posters or programs!" Chopin insisted.

"But we must spread the word." His friends said. "Otherwise how will you get a large audience?"

"I don't want a large audience!"

Chopin didn't want people to come because he was afraid of crowds. He hoped that maybe only a few friends would show up. He told George not to talk about the concert anymore, so the word wouldn't spread any further.

As the day approached, Chopin grew very worried. Suppose the audience didn't like his music?

"Then you'll just have to play without an audience." Said George.

What if the piano was out of tune? What if he played wrong notes?

"Maybe you should play on a pretend piano that makes no sound." Said George with a smile.

Suppose the candles fell over and set fire to the stage?

"Maybe you should play without candles." Said George. "A concert in the dark, on a piano that makes no noise, and without an audience."

Is that really a good concert?

Chopin knew that it wasn't. He was scared, but he knew if he didn't face his fears, no one would ever hear his beautiful music played just the way he liked to play it. If he didn't face his fears, people would forget about him as a pianist and composer. If he didn't face his fears, he wouldn't make money from the ticket sales, and that could mean no money for Christmas presents, or flowers, or paying the doctor, or buying purple gloves, or healthy food and low sugar chocolate or ice cream for the ice cream machine some nice ladies had given him!

If you had to choose between no ice cream and playing a concert in front of people, what would you do? Chopin decided to be brave.

At eight o'clock, Chopin's carriage pulled up to the house of Mr. Pleyel the piano maker. Chopin and George walked inside, down a long staircase lined with flowers. Chopin went to the middle of the room and sat down at the Pleyel Piano, his favorite kind of piano that was soft and delicate, perfect for playing his music. He looked into the big audience that made him so nervous. He saw the woman he loved, George, cheering him on. He saw his friend Franz Liszt in the audience too. In fact, he had a lot of friends in the audience! The audience wasn't something to be nervous of. They were on his side!

Chopin played preludes and mazurkas. He played his Ballade in F major. He played études and nocturnes. The audience applauded and asked him to play his music again and again!

"In two hours of two-handed tapping he pocketed six thousand and several hundred francs amidst ovations, encores and the stamping of the most beautiful women in Paris." George said.

Six thousand francs is a lot of money. Have you ever made a lot of money in one day? In the end, Chopin was glad that he gave his concert even though he had been so scared!

Here is the music Chopin played at his concert:

1. Prelude (Choose one of Chopin's 24 Preludes) – A prelude is a piece of music to play as an introduction. So it was the perfect start to Chopin's concert. Preludes are short. People didn't used to like music that was short, but Chopin changed that with his book of 24 preludes. The prelude set the mood for the rest of the concert. What do you think the mood was?

2. Ballade in F Major – Does this song begin slowly or fast? Does it stay that way? Listen for when the music changes. Chopin wrote this ballade in an abandoned monastery in Spain, surrounded by nature. While he was there, the weather changed from calm to stormy all the time. So he put stormy "episodes" throughout the otherwise calm ballade.

3. Mazurka (Choose one of Chopin's Mazurkas) – A mazurka is a Polish dance with skipping and hopping, led by the women. The man dances in the center, but the woman dances up and down the ballroom before coming back to him and dancing behind him. She finally comes back so they can dance together. Do you think this dance is fast or slow? Does it seem romantic, fun, or both?

4. Etude (You may listen to the Revolutionary Etude again) – An etude is full of exercises and workouts for the pianist, but the audience enjoys hearing them play something hard! So etudes became something to perform too, not just to use for practice. The etude (plus the fast and stormy sections of the ballade) must have taken great strength for Chopin to play. Franz Liszt noticed that Chopin looked worn out by the end of the concert, and was afraid he would fall over!

5. Nocturne (Nocturne 1 in e minor) – Nocturnes are songs about nighttime. They are relaxing and sometimes mysterious. Chopin published a book of nocturnes the year of his concert. Does this song remind you about the indoors during the night, or outside? What kind of a night do you think it is? Stormy and windy, or calm and quiet? In his nocturnes, Chopin used a technique called "rubato," which is speeding up or slowing down while playing. Listen to the song and see if you can hear it slow down and speed up again!

Note: Franz Liszt wrote about the concert in the paper. The full article is printed below, and while it is lengthy, certain sections may be chosen for continued reading.

"*Last Monday, at eight o'clock in the evening, the salons of Mr. Pleyel were splendidly lit; many crews brought incessantly to the bottom of a staircase covered with carpets and scented with flowers the most elegant women, the most fashionable young people, the most famous artists, the richest financiers, the greatest lords the most illustrious, an entire elite of society, an entire aristocracy of birth, fortune, talent, and beauty.*

A grand piano was opened on a platform; we huddled around; the nearest places were sought after; in advance we listened, we recollected ourselves, we told ourselves that we should not lose an agreement, a note, an intention, a thought of the one who was going to sit there. And it was right to be so greedy, attentive, religiously moved, because the one we expected, that we wanted to see, hear, admire, applaud, was not only a skillful virtuoso, a pianist expert in the art of making notes; he was not just an artist of great renown, it was all that and more than that, it was Chopin.

Coming to France about ten years ago, Chopin, in the crowd of pianists who at that time sprang up everywhere, did not fight to get first or second place. He made himself very little heard in public; the eminently poetic nature of his talent did not carry him there. Like those flowers which only open their fragrant chalices at night, he needed an atmosphere of peace and meditation to freely pour out the treasures of melody that rested in him. Music was his language; a divine language in which he expressed a whole order of feelings that only the few could understand. As well as to this other great poet, Mickiewicz, his compatriot and his friend, the muse of the fatherland dictated his songs to him, and the complaints of Poland borrowed with its accents I do not know what mysterious poetry which, for all those who have really felt, cannot be compared to anything. If less brilliance is attached to his name, if a halo less luminous girded his head, it is not that he could not have in him perhaps the same energy of thought, the same depth of feeling as the famous author of Konrad Wallenrod and Pilgrims ; but his own means of expressing himself were too limited, his human instrument too imperfect; he could not help using a piano to reveal himself entirely. Hence, if we are not mistaken, a dull and continuous suffering, a certain repugnance to communicating to the outside, a melancholy that escapes under appearances of gaiety, a whole individuality finally remarkable and endearing in the highest degree.

As we have said, it was only rarely, at very distant intervals, that Chopin made himself heard in public; but what would have been for others an almost certain cause of forgetfulness and obscurity, was precisely that which assured him a reputation superior to the caprices of fashion, and which sheltered him from rivalries, jealousies, and injustices. Chopin, left out of the excessive movement that, for some years, has been pushing against each other, and against each other, the performing artists from all points of the universe, has remained constantly surrounded by faithful followers, enthusiastic pupils, warm friends who, while guaranteeing him unhappy struggles and painful wrinkles, have not ceased to spread his works, and with them admiration for his genius and respect for his name. So, this exquisite celebrity, all of which is high, excellently aristocratic, has remained pure of all attack. A complete silence of criticism is already made around him, as if posterity had already come; and in the brilliant audience that ran to the poet, who was too silent for a long time, there was no reluctance, no restriction; all the mouths had only praise.

We will not undertake here a detailed analysis of Chopin's compositions. Without false research of the originality, it was him , as well in the style as in the design. To new thoughts he knew how to give a new form. This wild and abrupt thing which belonged to his country, found its expression in daring boldness, in strange harmonies, while the delicacy and the grace which held to his person revealed themselves in a thousand contours, in thousand ornaments of an incomparable fantasy.

In Monday's concert, Chopin had chosen those of his works that are more distant from classical forms. He played neither concerto, nor sonata, nor fantasy, nor variations, but preludes, studies, nocturnes and mazurkas. Addressing a society rather than an audience, he could with impunity show himself what he is, poet, mournful, profound, chaste and dreamy. He did not need to surprise or seize; he sought delicate sympathies rather than noisy enthusiasms. Let's say quickly that these sympathies did not fail him. From the first agreements he established a close communication between himself and his audience. Two studies and a ballad were requested again, and without the fear of adding more fatigue to the already great fatigue which betrayed itself on his pale face, one would have asked all the pieces of the program one by one.

Chopin's Preludes are compositions of an order quite apart. It is not only, as the title might suggest, pieces intended to be played as an introduction to other pieces; they are poetic preludes, analogous to those of a great contemporary poet, that cradle the soul in golden dreams, and elevate it to ideal regions. Admirable by their diversity, the work and knowledge found there are appreciable only at a scrupulous examination. Everything seems like first-rate, momentum, sudden arrival. They have the free and great pace that characterizes the works of genius.

What about the mazurkas, these little masterpieces so capricious and yet so complete?

A perfect sonnet is better than a long poem," said a man who was authoritative in the finest century of French letters. We should be tempted to apply to the Mazurkas the exaggeration of this axiom, and to say that for us, at least, many of them are worth very long operas.

After all the bravos lavished on the king of the party, Mr. Ernst knew how to get his just rewards. He played in a broad and grandiose style, with a passionate feeling and a purity worthy of the masters, an elegy that greatly impressed the audience.

Madame Damoreau, who had lent her charming participation to this fashionable concert , was, as usual, ravishing with perfection.

One more word before ending these few lines that the lack of time forces us to shorten.

The celebrity or success that crowns talent and genius is partly the product of happy circumstances. Lasting successes are rarely unfair, to tell the truth. However, since fairness is perhaps the rarest quality of the human mind, the result is that for some artists success remains below, while for others it goes beyond actual value. It has been noticed that in regular tides there is always a tenth wave stronger than the others; thus, in the train of the world, there are men who are carried by this tenth wave of fortune, and who go higher and further than others, their equals or even their superiors. The genius of Chopin was not helped by these particular circumstances. His success, though very great, remained below what he was to claim. However, we say it with conviction, Chopin has nothing to envy about anyone. Is not the most noble and the most legitimate satisfaction the artist can feel, to feel himself above his fame, superior even to his success, even greater than his glory?

F. LISZT."

VII.

Clara Can Do it Alone

Many children dream of running away from home to a big city. They think it will be a grand adventure. And maybe it will, if you wait until you're old enough to drive a car, and go to college or work at a job when you get there. Clara Wieck waited until she was seventeen.

When Clara was your age, she gave concerts. When she played piano, everyone listened: princes, poets, doctors, and even other pianists.

She traveled all over Austria, Germany, and France. People flocked to the box office and fought over tickets to her concerts. Bakers created desserts named after her. She made enough money to pay for a whole feast of food and a mountain of dresses. But Clara didn't get to see her money. It all went straight to Father, and he locked it away in a big chest and used it for himself.

Father was strict and demanding. Every day Clara practiced piano for two hours. And every day Father made her study violin, singing, French, English, music theory, and composition. Clara learned how to write beautiful music. She was given the highest musical honor in Austria: Royal and Imperial Chamber Virtuoso.

Still Father was not happy. He yelled at music critics, he shouted at conductors, and he argued with composers. But he never got mad at Clara, because Clara never did anything to upset him...

Until one day, when she was seventeen years old. She told him she wanted to get married. Father's rage burst out like a volcano. He ranted and raved. He fumed and insulted. His yelling made Clara cry.

I'll go to Paris without him, she thought.

Father said that was fine, she wouldn't last one day without him to plan her concerts. Clara set out to prove him wrong.

She packed her bags and left for her first concert tour without Father. It was snowing hard, but Clara traveled on. She didn't have enough money for the journey, but she played concerts on the way, and raised enough to get to Paris.

Paris was so big! There were nineteen theaters and three concert halls. There were concerts every night, by all kinds of musicians. And the pianists Thalberg, Chopin, and Liszt all lived in Paris. They were Clara's biggest competition.

Clara rolled up her sleeves and got to work.

Father used to plan her concerts. But this time, Clara did it herself. She met Mr. Cherubini, who was the principle of the Paris Conservatory.

Wouldn't it be a good idea to have a concert at the Conservatory?

Mr. Cherubini said yes!

Clara visited the Erard family who made musical instruments.

Could she give a concert in their big house?

They said yes too!

Father used to decide what piano Clara would use. This time, Mr. Erard and Mr. Pleyel both asked her to use their pianos. It was a hard decision, but Clara chose Mr. Pleyel's piano because she liked the sound better.

Father used to hire other musicians to play with Clara. Clara did this herself this time...and negotiated payment.

Father used to meet important music critics so they would write about Clara's concerts. This time Clara did it herself. She went to her friend Pauline Garcia who was living in Paris, and asked her to introduce her to all the musicians, composers, and writers.

Pauline was a famous singer, and knew everyone Clara should meet! Clara had dinner with the Bertin family, who published music. While she was there, she met another composer, Hector Berlioz. He agreed to write a review of her concert.

Father used to decide what music Clara would play. This time, Clara chose the music herself.

She played her Pirate Variations to enormous applause. The audience loved the music Clara had written.

Father used to collect the ticket money. But now, Clara collected the money.

"The musical lion of the moment!" said one newspaper.

"A most exquisite and artistic performance!" said another.

"Her compositions are ingenious!" said yet another.

"The crowned musician is Clara Wieck!"

Clara had established herself in Parisian society!

Father was not happy.

He wrote angry letters to Clara. He said he wouldn't give her money ever again. He said that she couldn't get married without his permission, and that if she tried, he would start a lawsuit.

Clara wrote to the Court of Appeals. She asked them to let her get married without Father's permission.

They said yes!

When Clara returned home, Father wouldn't let her in the house. All of her belongings were locked inside: her clothes, music, piano, and even her diary.

Father said she was no longer welcome there. He said all her money for the next five years belonged to him. And that she couldn't get married!

Yes I can, Clara thought. *I don't need you. I'll find somewhere else to live.*

Clara marched to her friend's house and stayed with her instead. Then she went to Berlin to live with her mother until she got married. She wondered if her mother would be upset that she ran away.

Her mother was proud. She was proud that Clara went to Paris alone so her father wouldn't take her money and use it for himself. And she was proud that Clara wrote to the court to tell them about the problem, so that they could help her.

Even though Clara loved Father, she knew that she would be happier living away from him. She still had her mother, and soon she would have a husband too.

What will I do to pass the time while I wait to get married, Clara wondered.

Clara decided to go on tour again! And this time...she took her mother with her.

Here's some music Clara wrote that you may like:

Bellini "Il Pirata" Variations – Clara went to see an opera about pirates! Then she went home and wrote this song about them. Variations are different versions of the same song played different ways: fast or slow, or high or low, or happy or sad! Listen to each variation and decide how they are different.

Art Song – Lorelai. This song is about a mermaid! Does she sound like a nice mermaid? Or a mermaid that likes to fight?

3 Romances for Violin and Piano – These duets were written for her friend Joseph Joachim, who played violin. Clara and Joachim gave hundreds of concerts together, with Clara on piano and Joachim on violin.

VIII.

Clara Saves the Day

It is important to obey your parents. Sometimes it makes things easier, like getting dinner on the table and keeping the house clean. Other times it may save your life if there is danger. In a city called Dresden, four little children had to obey their mother, and this is how it happened.

Clara was busy giving concerts. Her name was Clara Schumann now, because she had gotten married. Her husband's name was Robert Schumann. He composed and ran a newspaper about music. It was hard to make money writing music. But it was easy for Clara to make money by playing piano. So Clara was busy giving concerts.

Sometimes Clara and Robert wrote songs for each other. Robert wrote songs for Clara called "You are like a flower", and "You my soul, you my heart." Clara wrote a collection of songs and gave them to Robert for his birthday.

Clara and Robert had four children. Their three daughters were named Marie, Elise, and Julie. Then there was Baby Ludwig. He couldn't talk yet, but he cried a lot. The children all loved to hear their parents play the piano and sing at home.

But today there was no music in the Schumann house. Drums beat outside. The soldiers built barricades and hid behind them. Guns fired. It was Revolution!

Clara and Robert were not happy about the city's revolution. The streets were dangerous, so they stayed inside. Then the fighting got too close!

Baby Ludwig cried! Marie, Elise, and Julie hid!

Clara packed their belongings. She told Robert to get out of bed. She told Marie to be brave and to prepare for a special secret journey. When it was dark outside, Clara took Robert and Marie out the back door to escape!

Marie was seven, and knew how to be quiet and follow her parents. They snuck down the streets and kept to the shadows.

The revolutionists had a man standing lookout on the top of the Kreuzkirche. His name was Richard Wagner. He was friends with Franz Liszt and he knew the Schumanns. If he saw them leaving, would he raise the alarm?

No alarm was raised. They kept walking. They soon left the center of the city and came upon many houses. Marie looked around. There was no fighting! Clara told Marie that they would be safe here. They went inside one of the houses. Clara put her husband to bed because he was very sick.

Marie kept an eye on her sick father, but she was worried about Elise, Julie, and Baby Ludwig. They had been left behind with two servants to take care of them. Would they be okay?

Clara traveled back toward Dresden. She passed the quiet houses and heard the fighting get louder and louder. Some buildings were destroyed. The opera house was on fire!

Who would have set fire to the opera house? Was it Richard Wagner, who had been the director of the opera before joining the revolution? He made hand grenades for the revolutionists. Had he used some to burn down his own opera house? In the chaos, no one had seen it happen. It was a mystery.

Clara traveled on until she met soldiers who barred her way. They told her she couldn't go down those streets! They were fighting!

Clara would not take no for an answer. She had to rescue Elise, Julie, and Baby Ludwig! She walked right past the soldiers. She slipped past the road blocks. She snuck past the armed troops who were waiting to fight. Finally she ran back to her house.

Mommy!

Clara picked up Baby Ludwig and told Elise and Julie to follow her. They snuck past the armed troops. They slipped past the road blocks. And they walked right past the soldiers.

They kept walking, even though they were tired. Elise had just turned six and Julie was only four! They kept walking even though they were all afraid Baby Ludwig would cry!

But he didn't.

They reached the quiet houses safely. The Schumann family was together again! How brave all the children were! And how brave Mother Clara was!

And the whole time she was seven months pregnant with the newest member of the family! They named him Ferdinand.

Here are some songs by Robert and Clara Schumann that you may like:

By Robert:

Widmung (Dedication)

Du bust wie eine Blume (you are like a flower)

Du Ring am Meinen Finger (You ring on my finger)

By Clara:

Die Lorelei (The Mermaid)

Warum Willst du And're Fragen? (Why will you question others?)

Liebst du um Schonheit (if you love for beauty)

IX.

Richard Wagner on the Run

Last chapter we heard about a revolution called the Dresden May Uprising. Now we'll hear about what happened afterward to Richard Wagner, one of the revolutionists. More and more troops surrounded the city, and Wagner and his friends saw that their cause would soon be lost. Wagner ran away to Weimar to see his friend Franz Liszt.

Wagner sat in the back of the theater, in the darkness, watching Franz Liszt lead a performance of Wagner's opera "Tannhäuser." Wagner loved writing operas. He had written a new opera called "Lohengrin", but now that he had become a revolutionist, he was having trouble finding a theater that wanted to put it on.

Later that night, one of Wagner's friends burst into Liszt's living room and collapsed on the couch. A warrant had just been issued for Wagner's arrest! The police had already searched Wagner's house in Dresden, and knew he was missing. Wagner read the warrant.

"The Royal Kappelmeister Richard Wagner, of this place, who is described in detail below, is wanted for questioning in connection with his active part in the recent uprising here, but has not as yet been found. The police are therefore instructed to look out for him, and if he is found, to arrest him and communicate with me at once.

-Von Oppell, City Police Deputy

Wagner is 37-38 years old, of medium height, has brown hair, and wears glasses."

"Well, that could apply to a lot of people." Wagner said.

Franz was taking no chances. He borrowed sixty thalers from Princess Carolyne, gave them to Wagner, and sent him to the nearby village of Magdala. From there, Wagner walked six hours over the countryside to the town of Jena. When he arrived, Franz was waiting for him with a professor named Professor Widmann.

Franz told Wagner to take Professor Widmann's passport and use it to travel out of the country, to Bavaria, Paris, and Switzerland! Wagner took the passport. Now with his money and fake identification, he was ready to run!

When the border patrols asked him who he was, he said "Professor Widmann!" And showed them his passport. In this way he finally made it to the Swiss mountains.

What a journey!

Now Wagner didn't know what to do. No one would perform his music anymore! How would he get money?

Franz sent him money, and suggested he write some articles on music to earn more.

Wagner did, but...they were not nice articles. He hated the composers Meyerbeer and Mendelssohn because they never helped him out. So he wrote that their music was terrible, and that the reason it was terrible was because they were both Jewish! And therefore, Jewish Music was bad and no one should listen to it.

"Did you write this?" Franz cried.

"Of course it was me." Wagner shrugged. "Why do you even have to ask?"

Franz said no more about it, but he was angry. He was tired of fixing Wagner's messes. All Wagner wanted to do was start fights and blame other people for his problems. But of course Meyerbeer was not to blame for Wagner being unpopular. And no one can ever blame an entire race of people for their personal problems like Wagner tried to do. No, it was Wagner's own fault that he had ended up alone in Switzerland, and it was up to him to fix his own problems.

Wagner thought and thought until he remembered how Liszt's theater had put on Tannhauser. That gave him an idea.

"Liszt, perform my opera Lohengrin!" He said. "I trust it to no one but you!"

Franz Liszt agreed. He led 46 rehearsals of Lohengrin at the Weimar theater.

Wagner had another idea. He could come to Weimar to see the premiere...in disguise!

"No!" Franz said. "That would be illegal."

Instead, Wagner climbed to the top of a mountain in Lucerne, Switzerland. He went into a hotel and pulled out his pocket watch. The performance was starting! Far away in Weimar, Liszt tuned the orchestra, and the premiere of Wagner's opera "Lohengrin" began.

Wagner imagined the music he knew so well. He imagined the story coming to life. If only Wagner had made better choices and not gotten in trouble with the law, he would have been able to see his opera premiere! But he could only sit in silence and imagine.

He would stay in Switzerland for eleven years before he was finally pardoned. During that time, Franz Liszt worked tirelessly to make everyone like Wagner again. As you can imagine, it wasn't easy. But finally Wagner was allowed to come home. And then...

He married Liszt's daughter.

Here's some music Wagner wrote that you may like:

1. Wedding Song from Lohengrin – Brides still walk down the aisle to this wedding music from Wagner's opera "Lohengrin." We call it "Here comes the bride."

2. Pilgrim's Chorus from Tannhauser – This song is for a chorus of men and boys, and takes place at the end of the opera. Listen and decide whether the pilgrims start singing from up close or if they are far away! Do the singers get louder or softer as the song goes on?

Note: Wagner went on to lead a happy life and write many more operas. He never knew how damaging his comments against Meyerbeer and the Jewish people would become. Back then, Nazis didn't exist yet. Germany as a whole country didn't exist either, it was only separate little lands like Bavaria and Saxony. Jewish people were all over Europe, and were generally rich and successful, owning railroads and banks and publishing houses. Wagner himself said that nothing would ever happen to change how successful the Jewish people were. But the words he wrote when he was an angry exile, blaming other people for his problems, would have a lasting impact on the lives of his grandchildren.

Wagner's oldest grandson, Franz Beidler, married a Jewish girl named Ellen Gottschalk, daughter of a Jewish professor of medicine. When the Nazis took control of Germany, Franz fled to Zurich, Switzerland (the same city that Wagner had lived during his exile) with his Jewish wife and their small daughter Dagny, to protect them.

Wagner's grandsons and granddaughter Wieland, Wolfgang, and Verena made friends with Hitler and joined the Nazi party. Wolfgang's son Gottfried grew up to study Jewish history, founded the Post-Holocaust Discussion Group in 1992, and wrote books criticizing the members of his family who had joined the Nazis.

Wagner's granddaughter Friedeland Wagner spoke out against Hitler and ended up fleeing the country in 1939. She wrote anti-Nazi columns for the Daily Sketch newspaper in England before traveling to America and making anti-Nazi radio broadcasts.

Wagner's step-granddaughter Eva Busch was a cabaret singer. She lost her German citizenship and fled to Paris. When the Germans invaded Paris she was arrested and spent three and a half years in the Ravensbruck concentration camp.

Wagner died in 1881: more than fifty years before all this happened, and couldn't have known the same ideas in his angry article would one day cause so much pain for Europe and for his own grandchildren. Words spoken out of hurt and anger can cause lasting damage even if we never see that damage ourselves.

X.

Pauline the Peacemaker

Sometimes friends fight, and no matter what you do, you can't make them get along again. What do you do when two of your friends are fighting? You still want to be friends with both of them, but they might ask you to pick a side.

Pauline Viardot never picked sides.

Pauline's father was a famous opera singer: Manuel Garcia. Her older sister was a famous opera singer. So of course Pauline would become one too. When she was your age she took voice lessons from her father. She took piano lessons from a young man you might remember from earlier in the book: Franz Liszt. Franz and Pauline spent a lot of time at the piano together. Pauline liked piano better than singing! But everyone loved Pauline's voice, so she focused on that instead. Franz liked the music Pauline wrote, and said she was a good composer.

Besides being friends with Franz, Pauline was also friends with Clara, whom you have already met. "She is the most musical singer that exists," Clara said. Clara always had nice things to say about Pauline, and she thought maybe she was a better musician than she was. But Pauline thought Clara was the one who was wonderful!

Pauline loved her friends Clara and Franz, but she had even better friends. Her best friends were George Sand and Frederic Chopin. She visited them whenever she could. She laughed with George and played piano with Chopin. She and George nicknamed him "Chip-Chip," and Pauline called George "Ninoune." When Pauline was deciding who to marry, George was the one she asked for advice. When she had her first baby, George and Chopin were the ones who babysat while Pauline went out of town to sing!

Chopin had written piano pieces called mazurkas. Pauline started humming along as he played them. Then she had an idea. What if there were words to those melodies?

Chopin and Pauline, a sketch by Maurice Sand (George's son)

Chopin thought that was a great idea! So Pauline and Chopin sat down at the piano and worked on making his mazurkas into songs for singers! Pauline thought up all the words. Then she and Chopin changed some of the piano music to vocal music. Now it was a duet, and Pauline could sing the songs while Chopin played!

The three of them shared happy days together, and maybe they thought those days would never end. But something happened that made Pauline terribly sad.

George Sand and Frederic Chopin had a fight.

They didn't mean to. It was a small fight that came after a much bigger fight that George had with her daughter. Chopin loved both of them, and wanted to make sure George's daughter Solange was okay. But Solange only told him her side of the argument. She made her mother sound like a bad person. And then a worse thing happened: Chopin believed it.

George told Chopin not to visit her anymore. Maybe she thought he would feel sorry then, and apologize for thinking she was so bad.

But he never did.

Pauline loved both her friends George and Chopin, and listened sadly when Chopin explained what had happened.

"Now I can only help the daughter, because George refuses to talk to me." Chopin said.

Pauline listened sadly again when George told her what had happened. You see, Pauline visited Chopin alone. Then she visited George. She wrote letters to both of them. If she couldn't see both her friends together, she would see them one at a time, and try to make them feel better. They needed it, because now some of their other friends were spreading rumors and lies about the fight.

"In heaven's name, darling," Pauline told George, "Chopin is not changed toward you. He is still as kind and as devoted as ever — adoring you as he always has."

Pauline tried in vain to get her two friends to get along again. They had loved each other so much once, and maybe they would have gotten married. When Chopin thought of marriage that year, he could only think of George and how heartbroken he was.

Pauline was in England, singing for the queen. One day she was surprised to see Chopin. He was traveling to different countries to share his music, like Pauline was. But Chopin looked very sick. He was weaker than usual and coughing more.

Pauline went home and found a letter from George. George was worried about him. Was he okay? Was he really sick? Could Pauline check on him? Was he still angry with her?

He was, and he was not pleased that George had written to ask about him. There was only one thing now that Pauline could do to make Chopin feel better.

"I'm giving a concert," she said. "And I'm going to sing your mazurkas."

Chopin was tired, sick, and heartbroken, but the duets he and Pauline had written made him happy, if only for a moment. In England, Pauline was more famous than he was. So the program only said "Polish songs arranged by Madame Viardot." Only Pauline's name was printed, not his. But he told the printers that it was okay with him.

Chopin grew too sick to stay in England, and headed home to Paris. He rented an apartment that faced toward the sun and away from the wind, and prepared to face the cold winter.

When Pauline returned to Paris, some men knocked on her door.

"We would like you to sing at Chopin's funeral."

Pauline's heart sank in her chest. She wrote a letter to George.

"I was so grieved by the death of poor little Chopin that I didn't know where to start my letter. I am sure that you have also been similarly distressed, and that had you known that his end was so near you would have gone to press his hand one last time. I came to know of his death from strangers who had come to ask me very formally to participate in a Requiem, which was to be given at the Madeleine for Chopin. It is then that I realized how deep my affection was for him... He was a noble soul."

"My dear sweet one," George said. "I have been waiting for some time for the sad event to happen. I wrote to Chopin's sister in case he wished to see me. But there was no answer. People were lying to him until the very end. He forgot our nine years together. I forgive him. He loved the real me. It was a fake version of me that he hated. It wasn't his fault, it was his bad friends, and especially my daughter. She did everything she could to make me hate myself and wish I was dead."

It took much longer for George and her daughter to end their big fight, especially now that Chopin was gone. But they did make up in the end. Maybe if Chopin had not died so soon after he and George's fight, they would have made up too. But that's the thing about arguments. You may think they won't last, but someday it really could be too late to apologize. Your friends could move away, or switch scout troops or sports teams, or change their phone number or email. That's a reason why it's always best not to stay angry for long, but to say you're sorry.

Sadly, Chopin was not able to stay friends with both George and her daughter Solange when they fought. He chose a side—Solange—and once he did that, he entered into their argument too. That only made things worse for all of them.

But Pauline made a choice to stay friends with both George and Chopin. She refused to fight just because they were. And she refused to say unkind things about anyone who was fighting. Because she did this, she was able to help both of her friends when they were hurting.

So Chopin's response to fighting—to take sides—only ended in pain. Pauline's response to fighting—to be kind to both of them—made her friends feel better.

Pauline and George Sand stayed friends for years and years. When they were older, Pauline and her children came to visit George and her son and granddaughters. George asked Pauline to sing a special song "*Que Quieres Panchito.*" It brought back memories of those special times so long ago when Chopin was alive and playing his piano. Pauline finished singing, and George's eyes were full of a kind of painful joy. She said nothing, but Pauline saw that she was deeply moved.

"My Ninoune," she said gently, and comforted her.

George and Pauline missed Chopin, but they would always have their happy memories with him. And they would always have each other, too.

Pauline sang many operas and wrote some of her own. She wrote one opera when she was eighty! She also taught at the Paris Conservatory. When Clara Schumann heard Pauline's operas, she said "once more I have confirmation of what I have always said: that she is the most gifted woman I have ever met."

Here are some pieces that Pauline wrote:

1. Polish Songs by Pauline Viardot and Frederic Chopin

2. Cendrillon – Pauline wrote an opera of Cinderella! Have you ever seen a movie or a play of Cinderella? This opera has a wicked stepfather instead of a wicked stepmother. You can listen to the Fairy Godmother's Song, or Cinderella's song "There was once a handsome prince", they are both pretty!

3. La Dernier Sorcier – Pauline wrote this opera for her children to perform! Clara and Brahms went to it and loved it. Franz Liszt decided to premiere the opera professionally at his theater in Weimar! The opera has fairies and a magician in it!

XI.

Brahms's War

All the composers were friends and had mostly gotten along. But as time went on, some sad things happened.

Fanny Mendelssohn died. Her brother Felix had such a broken heart because of this that he died too. And we already heard that Chopin died in October of 1849, two years after Fanny and Felix died.

What other sad things could happen now?

Do you remember Clara and Robert Schumann, who had a big family they had to save when there was war in the city? Robert started seeing things that weren't there, hearing things than no one else heard, and making decisions like running away from home and jumping in a river. When the police fished him out, Clara realized Robert was sick. She took Robert to an asylum so nurses and doctors could take care of him.

Clara was alone with all her children. But she had a helper. He was a young composer friend of Robert's, and his name was Johannes Brahms. Brahms helped Clara around the house, visited Robert at the asylum, and babysat the children when Clara went on tour. He wrote the children a lullaby, and it became the most famous lullaby in the world. "Lullaby....and goodnight...go to sleep little baby..."

Clara and Brahms had something in common...they didn't like Liszt and Wagner's music. They thought music should stay the way it always had, and not change! Instead of traditional, classical music, Wagner's music was becoming modern!

Clara heard an opera Wagner wrote called "Tristan and Isolde."

"It's the most atrocious thing I've ever seen or heard in my life!" Clara wrote in her diary.

Clara liked her and Brahms's music better. So did many other people in Germany. Wagner and Liszt were called "the

New German School" because their ideas of chromatic harmony were new. Brahms and Clara's side was called "The Leipzig School" after the city where Robert Schumann and Felix Mendelssohn had written their music.

"My fingers itch to play anti-Liszt," Brahms muttered.

As for Clara, she used to like Franz Liszt back when they were younger. When they met they played music together every night. He once surprised her by giving her a brooch that he saw her admiring. She used to say he was a genius.

But now?

"He gives me the impression of a spoiled child." Clara said.

Why didn't Clara like Franz anymore? If you remember, in an earlier chapter about Franz, he came late to Clara's dinner party. Then he insulted Felix Mendelssohn. Clara said "I am done with Franz forever," and she meant it.

She was also done with Franz when he refused to give her angry father free tickets to his concert.

She was done with Franz when his piano student sued her father in court for saying bad things about him.

She had once written in her diary that it was impossible to be angry with Franz because he was so kind. But now

Clara's heart was sad because she had lost Robert, and she found it easy to be angry!

Brahms had an idea. He wrote a piece of paper against Liszt and his followers, and tried to get everyone to sign their names below it. The paper called Liszt's followers "rank, miserable weeds growing from Liszt-like fantasias." But the paper was leaked to the press early and the newspapers made fun of Brahms instead!

Poor Brahms! He learned the hard way not to make fun of others! He kept his opinions to himself after that. He focused on his music, and his success grew. So did his beard. He wrote symphonies, violin concertos, and Hungarian dances. Brahms was hailed as the national composer, and given an honorary doctorate.

Wagner was jealous. Brahms wasn't insulting Liszt anymore, but Wagner never needed an excuse to say mean things.

Why do they think of Brahms as a national composer, thought Wagner angrily. Better than me? But I'm the one writing operas based on our best fairy tales! Brahms doesn't write music about Germany. Brahms writes Hungarian dances and he isn't even Hungarian! He just does it for money!

"I know of some famous composers who in their concert masquerades don the disguise of a street-singer one day, the hallelujah periwig of Handel the next, the dress of a Jewish Czardas-fiddler another time, and then again the guise of a highly respectable symphony dressed up as Number Ten." Wagner said smugly.

In his mind, he was the true national composer. And Brahms's first symphony was just a copy of Beethoven: a fake Beethoven Symphony Number Ten.

The "war" between Wagner and Brahms got worse and worse.

Brahms became music director of a big concert hall in Vienna and he made sure no music by Liszt or Wagner was ever performed there.

Wagner's followers celebrated the anniversary of the newspaper Robert had started…and didn't invite Clara.

Brahms's piano concerto premiered in Hamburg and was met with boos and hisses! Liszt's symphonies and symphonic poems were booed too, by Brahms's followers!

Was all the fighting worth it? Everyone's music was getting booed. And secretly…ever so secretly…

Brahms actually liked Wagner's music.

"I am the best of the Wagnerians!" he said.

If he liked Wagner, why did he call him a weed? Well, Brahms loved Clara Schumann, even though they never got married. And Clara didn't like Wagner. So Brahms insulted him too.

Did the war ever end? Maybe it did. Or maybe it still goes on today. Your grandparents have their own style of music they like. And you have yours. Yours is probably newer, and they might not like it. But you can help stop the war by listening to the many styles of music and learning what people like about them.

Here's some music Brahms wrote that you may like...

1. Brahms's Lullaby – Have you heard this lullaby before? Clara's little children loved it!

2. Hungarian Dance Number 5 – Brahms wrote popular dance music, and this is one that the public loved most of all. This song has loud and soft parts, slow and fast parts! That makes it fun to dance to!

3. Symphony Number 1 – Wagner said this symphony sounded too much like Beethoven. Do you think so? Maybe Brahms *wanted* to sound like Beethoven.

(Siegfried Wagner with his sisters and stepsisters)

XII.

A Festival of Operas

Isolde, Eva, and Siegfried Wagner loved to play dress up! They loved playing with their big black dogs and running in the grass at their house called Villa Wahnfried. They loved fairy tales. And they loved their father's operas.

While Siegfried was growing up, his parents were building a theater. A big theater! And when it was finished, Daddy would premiere his operas!

Siegfried's father was named Richard Wagner. Wagner wrote many exciting operas and he named his children after each opera! Isolde was named after the princess from his opera "Tristan and Isolde," Eva was named after a character in "Die Meistersinger von Nurnburg," and Siegfried was named after Daddy's biggest opera of all: a story four operas long! The operas were "The Rhinegold", The Valkyrie," "Siegfried," and "Twilight of the gods." The whole thing together was called "The Ring of the Nibelungs."

Siegfried was excited for the operas to be performed, but first they needed to finish building the theater. Daddy's theater would be different than any others. It would be special.

Daddy didn't want the orchestra on stage during his operas. He wanted them hidden! So they needed to dig a pit below the stage big enough for the whole orchestra to fit inside!

The seats needed to be in rows all together instead of looking like little rooms called "stalls."

The room had to be shaped just right so the orchestra's sound from the pit floated out to the audience while the singer's sound floated out from the stage.

And finally, the theater lights needed to turn all the way off when the operas started!

(Wagner's Theater)

Whew! What a lot of work! Finally the theater was finished. Now the Wagner family needed to invite an audience to come see the operas! It would be an opera festival!

Wagner invited everyone to his festival! He invited princes and kings, countesses and duchesses! He invited journalists and reporters. And he invited composers.

The guests arrived! Bruckner, Saint-Saens, and Grieg all came, excited to hear the music.

Wagner invited Clara and Brahms. They didn't come. They sat at home, sure that the music would be no good. They still considered themselves at war with Wagner.

It was too bad. They missed the Emperor of Brazil! And King Wilhelm of Prussia! Wagner dressed in his finest clothes and drove his carriage to the train station to greet King Wilhelm. The crowd cheered!

A reporter for the Russian newspaper ran around the festival interviewing the guests! His name was Piotr Tchaikovsky.

And someone else come, a dearer guest to Siegfried than any royalty.

"Grandfather!" Siegfried shouted.

It was Siegfried's grandfather: Franz Liszt!

Franz Liszt's brown hair was now grey, but his clear eyes twinkled merrily just as they used to in his younger days. Franz Liszt used to be rich and famous and bang on pianos, but not anymore. He gave away many of his belongings and became a priest! Now he wore a black robe with a cross necklace. He was happy to come to his daughter and son-in-law's festival of operas! And he was happy to see his grandchildren.

The crowd of guests marched up the hill from the town center to the theater. The audience crowded into their seats. The lights went out, and the music started in the hidden pit. The violins and flutes reminded Siegfried of the running water of the Rhine. Onstage, the water fairies swam in the air with the help of ropes!

(The Rhinemaidens from Das Rheingold, 1876)

"At four o'clock sharp a loud fanfare is sounded, and the whole crowd rushes into the theatre. Within five minutes everyone is seated. The fanfare is repeated again, the conversational hum dies down spontaneously, the gaslights illuminating the auditorium

suddenly go out, the whole theatre is plunged into total darkness, and from the depths of the hidden orchestra pit below there swell up the beautiful sounds of the prelude. The curtain rises, and the performance begins." –Tchaikovsky

The first opera was over and it was time for something to eat. There were so many people that the restaurants were crowded and it was hard to get food! Siegfried and his sisters were glad they could eat at home with their parents and Grandfather Franz.

"I met one lady, the wife of a very high-ranking figure in Russia, who did not once have lunch during her whole stay in Bayreuth — coffee was her only source of nourishment." –Tchaikovsky

The next day, the Valkyries took the stage. They were warrior women whose horses rode on the clouds. In the pit, the horns and trumpets bellowed. "Hi-ya-to-ho! Hi-ya-to-ho!" The Valkyries sang. The audience loved the Ride of the Valkyries!

(Amalie Materna as Brunnhilde the Valkyrie in 1876)

Then came the opera Siegfried was most excited about! The opera called "Siegfried!" He was not disappointed. It had a dragon in it! The mechanical dragon rolled onstage and blew smoke from its mouth. The hero Siegfried fought it and saved the day!

On the last day of the festival, the audience filed into the theater, hot and hungry, to see the opera "Twilight of the gods". The orchestra played a beautiful song, and Siegfried recognized it as the song his Daddy had written for Mommy for Christmas! All the musicians had quietly come upstairs to surprise her with their playing. Now the whole audience could enjoy the song too.

At the end of the opera, the gods' secret kingdom went up in flames! Siegfried was proud of his father's special stage effects.

"After the final chord of the closing scene in the last opera of the cycle had died away, the audience called for Wagner. He walked onstage and made a small speech, which concluded with the following words: "You have seen what we can do — now it's up to you to want. And if you want, then we shall have an art!"

– Tchaikovsky

The festival was over! Now what? The Wagner family decided to do the festival again! It became a yearly tradition.

When Wagner died, it became Siegfried's festival, and he was in charge. Then Siegfried's children grew up and ran the festival. Then their children ran it!

To this day, people from all over the world come to Wagner's theater to attend the annual opera festival. It is hard to get tickets because they sell so fast. And it's still hard to get food in the busy restaurants. But when people sit in the dark theater and hear the beautiful melodies, all the troubles of the outside world fade away.

(Siegfried and his father Richard Wagner)

Did You Know?

Do the theater's special plans seem familiar? That's because the theaters today are all modeled after the one Siegfried's father was building! It was the first of its kind, and people liked it so much that they made all theaters with dim lights and orchestra pits!

Wagner invented themes for the places and characters in his operas. Those themes are called "leitmotif," and they play whenever a character comes onstage. When movies were invented, composers used leitmotif to write film music! Some film music that uses themes for characters and places are "Star Wars" by John Williams and "The Lord of the Rings" by Howard Shore.

Tchaikovsky didn't just write reviews for the Russian newspapers, he also wrote his own music! During Wagner's opera festival he was working on a ballet called "Swan Lake." He later wrote "The Nutcracker."

Here's some music by Wagner that you may like:

3. Das Rheingold Prelude – Can you hear the running water? During this music, the ladies on stage use ropes to rise into the air! But the audience uses their imagination to picture them as swimming water fairies!
4. Ride of the Valkyries (Die Walkure) – In this music, Brunhilde and her magical sisters fly through the clouds on their horses, bringing fallen soldiers to heaven. Are the clouds peaceful, or do you think there's a storm?

Epilogue

Now we have come to the end of the Romantic Composers and their stories. Let us leave them here to finish the rest of their happy lives: Franz Liszt and Richard Wagner are in the new theater, watching Wagner's operas. Pauline Viardot and Clara Schumann are best friends living next door to each other in Baden, and Clara comes to all of Pauline's operas. Clara still plays concerts, and even though she and Brahms don't like Wagner, Clara has promised she will watch Die Walkure again and play closer attention to see why people like it. George Sand still misses Chopin, but she sits quietly in her country house with his picture on her desk and writes books. Pauline still visits her. Pauline visits Franz Liszt too, even though she has different musical ideas than him. Music changed so much from when these fine musicians were children! And their lives helped change it. When we listen to their music, it's like opening a portal to the past. Let's never stop listening!

Research:

Clara Schumann, the Artist and the Woman, by Nancy B. Reich

Franz Liszt, Volume 2 the Weimar Years, by Alan Walker

The Complete Correspondence of Fryderyk Chopin, by Fryderyk Chopin

Correspondence of Franz Liszt and Richard Wagner Volume I and II

Franz Liszt Letters Volumes I, II, III, by Franz Liszt

George Sand Letters Volumes I, II, III, by George Sand

About the Author

Hannah Hoyt holds multiple degrees from Berklee College of Music and is an active composer, operatic soprano, researcher, and music educator. She teaches 30+ children a week in private lessons and group settings in North Carolina.

Her choral and orchestral compositions and arrangements have been performed by Myers Park Presbyterian Church, the Audire Soundtrack Choir and Orchestra, Fahrenheit 402 Chamber Ensemble, the SSP Orchestra, the a cappella group "PXL8," and Cool Springs United Methodist Church. She has received awards from the Symphony Guild of Charlotte and Community School of the Arts, and has been a musical guest/panelist at DragonCon, Northeast Trek Con, and The Charlotte Mason Institute conferences. Her music can be heard in the soundtracks to "Mondrian: Abstraction in Beauty" (VG), "Ariel" (GenCon Film Festival) "Think it Thru" (INSP) and the webseries "In Earnest."

As a soprano soloist she has performed internationally in Germany, England, and Greece as well as at Boston Symphony Hall. She is a company member of Opera Carolina and the artistic director of the Little Opera Company.

Other publications include "The Complete Correspondence of Wagner and Liszt Volume I" available on Amazon Kindle, "Christmas With Chopin" (2018) and the first English translation of "Rustic Legends" by George Sand (2017).

Made in the USA
Las Vegas, NV
25 August 2023

76616739R00059